This Journal Belongs To

CPSIA information can be obtained
at www.ICGtesting.com
Printed in the USA
BVOW04s0246181217
503089BV00010B/541/P